# Rosary
## of Praise

# Rosary of Praise

## A Scriptural Rosary Based on John Paul II's Rosary Meditation

### Larry & Connie London

Our Sunday Visitor Publishing Division
Our Sunday Visitor, Inc.
Huntington, Indiana 46750

*Nihil Obstat*
Rev. Michael Heintz
*Imprimatur*
John M. D'Arcy, Bishop of Fort Wayne-South Bend
May 15, 2003

The *nihil obstat* and *imprimatur* are official declarations that a book
is free of doctrinal or moral error. No implication is contained therein
that those who have granted the *nihil obstat* and *imprimatur* agree
with the content, opinions, or statements expressed.

# Contents

# Introduction

"*And* a voice came out from the throne, saying: Give praise to our God, all ye his servants; and you that fear him, little and great" (Apocalypse 19:5). This call to praise is by no means unique. From the first book to the last, the Holy Scriptures persistently echo the necessity of our praising the Almighty.

It seems the importance of praise cannot be overstated (see Ephesians 1:4a, 6a). In other words, we were created to praise the Almighty!

Incorporating praise into our prayers might sometimes seem strange; and yet through persistence, many have found it a powerful means of edification. Praise has often been called the highest form of prayer, but rather than comparing praise to blessing, petition, intercession, or thanksgiving, we might consider the words of the *Catechism of the Catholic Church* and incorporate praise into all our prayers to enhance whatever form of prayer we are using. The *Catechism* says:

"Praise embraces the other forms of prayer and carries them toward him who is its source and goal: the 'one God, the Father, from whom are all things and for whom we exist' [1 Cor 8:6]" (No. 2639).

One might ask, "How do I praise? What should I say?" These are common questions, but we can rejoice in the fact that God in His great goodness did not leave us without either words of praise or a prayer partner. The Holy Scriptures contain many glorious passages of praise that we might raise to the Almighty, and Our Lord has provided us with the best possible prayer partner — His mother, Mary. Praising with God's own Word and the Blessed Virgin's intercession, we can feel confident that our prayers will be pleasing to the Father.

The *Rosary of Praise* blends a wide selection of the greatest Scriptures of praise with scriptural meditations on the Rosary mysteries to form an uplifting scriptural Rosary of praise. This weekly scriptural Rosary incorporates the Holy Father's new Luminous Meditations and follows his recommended sequence of mysteries throughout the week. There is a corresponding verse for each

---

of the fifty Hail Marys (a rosarium) prayed daily. Each verse has been divided with a slash, so that they may be easily proclaimed in a two-part fashion. The *Douay-Rheims Bible* was chosen because of the unparalleled suitability of its elegant language for use in praising the Almighty.

May our Holy Mother lead all praising hearts more deeply into the love of the Father, and of the Son, and of the Holy Spirit. Amen.

# Monday's
# Joyful Mysteries

# *Monday's First Joyful Mystery*
## THE ANNUNCIATION

*— Our Father —*

And in the sixth month, the angel Gabriel was
sent from God into a city of Galilee, called
Nazareth, /
To a virgin espoused to a man whose name was
Joseph, of the house of David; and the
virgin's name was Mary.　　LUKE 1:26-27

*— Hail Mary —*

For I will behold thy heavens, the works of thy
fingers: the moon and the stars . . . /
What is man that thou art mindful of him?
　　　　　　　　　　　　PSALM 8:4-5A

*— Hail Mary —*

And the angel being come in, said unto her: /
Hail, full of grace, the Lord is with thee:
blessed art thou among women.　　LUKE 1:28

---

*— Hail Mary —*

Who is like to thee, among the strong, O Lord? /
who is like to thee, glorious in holiness, terrible
and praise-worthy, doing wonders?

EXODUS 15:11

*— Hail Mary —*

Who having heard, was troubled at his saying, /
and thought with herself what manner of
salutation this should be.

LUKE 1:29

*— Hail Mary —*

The Lord *is* my strength and my praise, and he
is become salvation to me: /
he *is* my God, and I will glorify him: the God
of my father, and I will exalt him.

EXODUS 15:2

*— Hail Mary —*

Therefore the Lord himself shall give you a sign.
Behold a virgin shall conceive, and bear a
son, /
and his name shall be called Emmanuel.

ISAIAS 7:14

*— Hail Mary —*

I will give praise to thee, O Lord, with my
    whole heart: /
 I will relate all thy wonders.       Psalm 9:2

*— Hail Mary —*

He shall be great and shall be called the Son of
    the most High; /
And of his kingdom there shall be no end.
                               Luke 1:32a, 33

*— Hail Mary —*

I will be glad, and rejoice in thee: /
 I will sing to thy name, O thou most high.
                                 Psalm 9:3

*— Hail Mary —*

*— Glory Be —*

---

# *Monday's Second Joyful Mystery*
## THE VISITATION

*— Our Father —*

And Mary rising up in those days, went into the
hill country with haste into a city of Juda. /
And she entered into the house of Zachary, and
saluted Elizabeth.                    LUKE 1:39-40

*— Hail Mary —*

But as for me in the multitude of thy mercy,
I will come into thy house; /
I will worship towards thy holy temple,
in thy fear.                    PSALM 5:8

*— Hail Mary —*

And it came to pass, that when Elizabeth heard
the salutation of Mary, /
the infant leaped in her womb.    LUKE 1:41A

*— Hail Mary —*

And to him my soul shall live: /
and my seed shall serve him.

PSALM 21:31

*— Hail Mary —*

And Elizabeth was filled with the Holy [Spirit]*:
    And she cried out with a loud voice, and
    said: /
Blessed art thou among women, and blessed is
    the fruit of thy womb.      LUKE 1:41B-42

*— Hail Mary —*

I will declare thy name to my brethren: /
in the midst of the church will I praise thee.

PSALM 21:23

*— Hail Mary —*

. . . that the mother of my Lord should come
    to me? /
For behold as soon as the voice of thy
    salutation sounded in my ears, the infant in
    my womb leaped for joy.      LUKE 1:43B-44

*— Hail Mary —*

* "Ghost" in the original translation

Praise the Lord, O Jerusalem: praise thy God,
    O Sion. /
Because he . . . blessed thy children within thee.
                                    PSALM 147:12-13

— *Hail Mary* —


And blessed art thou that . . . believed, /
    because those things shall be accomplished that
    were spoken to thee by the Lord.
                                    LUKE 1:45

— *Hail Mary* —


Behold the eyes of the Lord are on them that
    fear him: /
and on them that hope in his mercy.
                                    PSALM 32:18

— *Hail Mary* —

— *Glory Be* —

# *Monday's Third Joyful Mystery*
## THE NATIVITY

— *Our Father* —

And it came to pass, that in those days there
went out a decree from Caesar Augustus, that
the whole world should be enrolled. /
And all went to be enrolled, every one into his
own city.                                    LUKE 2:1, 3

— *Hail Mary* —

Hear, O ye kings, give ear, o ye princes: It is I, it
is I, that will sing to the Lord, /
I will sing to the Lord the God of Israel.
                                              JUDGES 5:3

— *Hail Mary* —

And Joseph also went up from Galilee, out of
the city of Nazareth into Judea, to the city of
David, /

---

To be enrolled with Mary his espoused wife,
who was with child. LUKE 2:4A, 5

*— Hail Mary —*

The mountains melted before the face of the
Lord, /
and Sinai before the face of the Lord the God
of Israel. JUDGES 5:5

*— Hail Mary —*

And it came to pass that when they were there, /
her days were accomplished, that she should be
delivered. LUKE 2:6

*— Hail Mary —*

For thou lightest my lamp, O Lord: /
O my God enlighten my darkness.

PSALM 17:29

*— Hail Mary —*

And she brought forth her firstborn son, and
wrapped him up in swaddling clothes, /
and laid him in a manger; because there was no
room for them in the inn. LUKE 2:7

*— Hail Mary —*

The Lord liveth, and blessed be my God, /
  and let the God of my salvation be exalted:
PSALM 17:47

*— Hail Mary —*

And the Word was made flesh, and dwelt
  among us, (and we saw his glory, /
the glory as it were of the only begotten of the
  Father,) full of grace and truth.
JOHN 1:14

*— Hail Mary —*

Therefore will I give glory to thee, O Lord, /
  among the nations, and I will sing a psalm to
  thy name.      PSALM 17:50

*— Hail Mary —*

*— Glory Be —*

---

# *Monday's Fourth Joyful Mystery*
## THE PRESENTATION

*— Our Father —*

And after the days of her purification, according
to the law of Moses, were accomplished, they
carried him to Jerusalem, to present him to
the Lord: /
And to offer a sacrifice, according as it is
written in the law of the Lord, a pair of
turtledoves, or two young pigeons:
LUKE 2:22, 24

*— Hail Mary —*

Out of the mouth of infants and of sucklings
thou ... perfected praise, /
Thou ... subjected all things under his feet:
PSALM 8:3A, 8A

*— Hail Mary —*

---

And behold there was a man in Jerusalem
named Simeon, and this man was just and
devout, /
waiting for the consolation of Israel; and the
Holy [Spirit]* was in him.           LUKE 2:25

— *Hail Mary* —


My God is my helper, and in him will I put
my trust. /
My protector and the horn of my salvation,
and my support.           PSALM 17:3B-C

— *Hail Mary* —


And he came by the Spirit into the temple.
And when his parents brought in the child
Jesus, to do for him according to the custom
of the law, /
He also took him into his arms, and blessed
God . . .           LUKE 2:27-28

— *Hail Mary* —


* "Ghost" in the original translation

My heart ... rejoiced in the Lord, and my horn
   is exalted in my God: /
There is none holy as the Lord is: for there is no
   other beside thee, and there is none strong
   like our God.                    1 KINGS 2:1A, 2

— *Hail Mary* —


... dismiss thy servant, O Lord, according to
   thy word in peace; /
Because my eyes have seen thy salvation,
                                   LUKE 2:29-30

— *Hail Mary* —


Thou ... turned for me my mourning into joy: /
O Lord my God, I will give praise to thee
   for ever.                       PSALM 29:12A,13B

— *Hail Mary* —


A light to the revelation of the Gentiles, /
   and the glory of thy people Israel.
                                   LUKE 2:32

— *Hail Mary* —

As for my God, his way is undefiled: the words
   of the Lord are fire tried: /
he is the protector of all that trust in him.

PSALM 17:31

*— Hail Mary —*

*— Glory Be —*

# *Monday's Fifth Joyful Mystery*
## THE FINDING OF JESUS IN THE TEMPLE

*— Our Father —*

And when he was twelve years old, they going
   up into Jerusalem, /
according to the custom of the feast,
LUKE 2:42

*— Hail Mary —*

The law of the Lord is unspotted, converting
   souls: /
the testimony of the Lord is faithful, giving
   wisdom to little ones.     PSALM 18:8
*— Hail Mary —*

And having fulfilled the days, when they
   returned, the child Jesus remained in
   Jerusalem; /
and his parents knew it not.     LUKE 2:43
*— Hail Mary —*

---

God, his way *is* immaculate, the word of the
Lord is tried by fire: /
he is the shield of all that trust in him.

2 KINGS 22:31

— *Hail Mary* —

And thinking that he was in the company, they
came a day's journey, /
and sought him among their kinsfolks and
acquaintance.

LUKE 2:44

— *Hail Mary* —

He bowed the heavens, and came down: and
darkness was under his feet. /
And he rode upon the cherubims, and flew:
and slid upon the wings of the wind.

2 KINGS 22:10-11

— *Hail Mary* —

And not finding him, they returned into
Jerusalem, seeking him. And it came to pass,
that, after three days, /

they found him in the temple, sitting in the
   midst of the doctors, hearing them, and
   asking them questions.          LUKE 2:45-46
           *— Hail Mary —*


For thou art my lamp, O Lord: /
   and thou, O Lord, wilt enlighten my darkness.
                              2 KINGS 22:29
           *— Hail Mary —*


And all that heard him /
   were astonished at his wisdom and his answers.
                              LUKE 2:47
           *— Hail Mary —*


Let all the earth fear the Lord, /
   and let all the inhabitants of the world be in
   awe of him.                  PSALM 32:8
           *— Hail Mary —*


           *— Glory Be —*

# Tuesday's Sorrowful Mysteries

# Tuesday's First Sorrowful Mystery
## THE AGONY IN THE GARDEN

*— Our Father —*

And going out, he went, according to his
custom, to the mount of Olives. /
And his disciples also followed him.

LUKE 22:39

*— Hail Mary —*

Do not multiply to speak lofty things, boasting:
let old matters depart from your mouth: /
for the Lord is a God of all knowledge, and to
him are thoughts prepared.     1 KINGS 2:3

*— Hail Mary —*

And when he was come to the place,
he said to them: /
Pray, lest ye enter into temptation.

LUKE 22:40

*— Hail Mary —*

But the salvation of the just is from the Lord,
and he is their protector in the time of
trouble. /
and he will rescue them from the wicked, and
save them, because they have hoped in him.
PSALM 36:39, 40B

*— Hail Mary —*

And taking with him Peter and the two sons of
Zebedee, /
he began to grow sorrowful and to be sad.
MATTHEW 26:37

*— Hail Mary —*

He will keep the feet of his saints, and the
wicked shall be silent in darkness, /
because no man shall prevail by his own
strength.
1 KINGS 2:9

*— Hail Mary —*

And when he was gone forward a little, he fell
flat on the ground; /
and he prayed, that if it might be, the hour
might pass from him.
MARK 14:35

*— Hail Mary —*

Our God is our refuge and strength: a helper in
    troubles, which have found us exceedingly. /
Therefore we will not fear, when the earth
    shall be troubled; and the mountains shall
    be removed into the heart of the sea.

PSALM 45:2-3

*— Hail Mary —*

. . . he went and prayed, saying: My Father,
    if this chalice may not pass away, /
but I must drink it, thy will be done.

MATTHEW 26:42

*— Hail Mary —*

The adversaries of the Lord shall fear him: and
    upon them shall he thunder in the heavens. /
The Lord shall judge the ends of the earth, and
    he shall give empire to his king, and shall
    exalt the horn of his Christ.

1 KINGS 2:10

*— Hail Mary —*

*— Glory Be —*

---

# *Tuesday's Second Sorrowful Mystery*
## THE SCOURGING AT THE PILLAR

*— Our Father —*

And when morning was come, all the chief
　　priests and ancients of the people took
　　counsel against Jesus, that they might put
　　him to death. /
And they brought him bound, and delivered
　　him to Pontius Pilate the governor.

MATTHEW 27:1-2

*— Hail Mary —*

I will call on the Lord who is worthy to be
　　praised: /
and I shall be saved from my enemies.

2 KINGS 22:4

*— Hail Mary —*

---

And Pilate asked him, saying: /
Art thou the king of the Jews?

LUKE 23:3A

— *Hail Mary* —

For the Lord is high, terrible: /
a great king over all the earth.

PSALM 46:3

— *Hail Mary* —

Pilate therefore said to him: Art thou a king
then? Jesus answered: /
For this was I born, and for this came I into
the world; that I should give testimony
to the truth.          JOHN 18:37A, C

— *Hail Mary* —

The voice of the Lord *is* in power; /
the voice of the Lord in magnificence.

PSALM 28:4

— *Hail Mary* —

But you have a custom that I should release one
unto you at the pasch: /

---

will you, therefore, that I release unto you the
   king of the Jews?                    JOHN 18:39

— *Hail Mary* —


Gather ye together his saints to him: /
who set his covenant before sacrifices.

PSALM 49:5

— *Hail Mary* —


But they cried again, saying: Crucify him,
   crucify him. And he said to them the third
   time: /
I find no cause of death in him. I will chastise
   him therefore, and let him go.

LUKE 23:21-22A, C

— *Hail Mary* —


And the heavens shall declare his justice: /
for God is judge.                    PSALM 49:6


— *Hail Mary* —


— *Glory Be* —

# Tuesday's Third Sorrowful Mystery
## THE CROWNING WITH THORNS

— *Our Father* —

Then the soldiers of the governor taking Jesus
   into the hall, /
gathered together unto him the whole band;
MATTHEW 27:27

— *Hail Mary* —

Declare his glory among the Gentiles: /
  his wonders among all people.
1 PARALIPOMENON 16:24

— *Hail Mary* —

And stripping him, /
  they put a scarlet cloak about him.
MATTHEW 27:28

— *Hail Mary* —

---

Therefore will I give thanks to thee, O Lord, /
among the Gentiles, and will sing to thy name.
2 KINGS 22:50

*— Hail Mary —*

And platting a crown of thorns, they put it
    upon his head, /
and a reed in his right hand.
MATTHEW 27:29A

*— Hail Mary —*

The Lord shall reign /
for ever and ever.
EXODUS 15:18

*— Hail Mary —*

And bowing the knee before him, they mocked
    him, /
saying: Hail, king of the Jews.
MATTHEW 27:29B

*— Hail Mary —*

Sing praises to our God, sing ye: sing praises to
    our king, sing ye. /
For God is the king of all the earth: sing ye
    wisely.                                    PSALM 46:7-8


*— Hail Mary —*


And spitting upon him, /
    they took the reed, and struck his head.
                                        MATTHEW 27:30

*— Hail Mary —*


The bruised reed he shall not break, and
    smoking flax he shall not quench: /
he shall bring forth judgment unto truth.
                                        ISAIAS 42:3

*— Hail Mary —*

*— Glory Be —*

# Tuesday's Fourth Sorrowful Mystery
## THE CARRYING OF THE CROSS

— *Our Father* —

And after they had mocked him, they took off
the cloak from him, /
and put on him his own garments, and led him
away to crucify him.          MATTHEW 27:31
— *Hail Mary* —

In thee, O Lord, have I hoped, let me never be
confounded: /
deliver me in thy justice.          PSALM 30:1
— *Hail Mary* —

And going out, they found a man of Cyrene,
named Simon: /
him they forced to take up his cross.
                              MATTHEW 27:32
— *Hail Mary* —

---

Praise ye his holy name: /
let the heart of them rejoice, that seek the Lord.

1 PARALIPOMENON 16:10

*— Hail Mary —*


And there followed him a great multitude of
    people, and of women, /
who bewailed and lamented him.

LUKE 23:27

*— Hail Mary —*


Seek ye the Lord, and his power: /
seek ye his face evermore.

1 PARALIPOMENON 16:11

*— Hail Mary —*


But Jesus turning to them, said: Daughters of
    Jerusalem, weep not over me; /
but weep for yourselves, and for your children.

LUKE 23:28

*— Hail Mary —*

Remember his wonderful works, . . . Remember
    for ever his covenant: /
the word, which he commanded to a thousand
    generations.

1 PARALIPOMENON 16:12A, 15

— Hail Mary —


For if in the green wood they do these things, /
what shall be done in the dry?

LUKE 23:31

— Hail Mary —


For the Lord is great and exceedingly to be
    praised: and he is to be feared above all
    gods. /
For all the gods of the nations are idols:
    but the Lord made the heavens.

1 PARALIPOMENON 16:25-26


— Hail Mary —

— Glory Be —

# Tuesday's Fifth Sorrowful Mystery
## THE CRUCIFIXION

*— Our Father —*

And when they were come to the place which is
called Calvary, they crucified him there; /
and the robbers, one on the right hand, and the
other on the left.                    LUKE 23:33

*— Hail Mary —*

Let all that seek thee rejoice and be glad in
thee: /
and let such as love thy salvation say always:
The Lord be magnified.          PSALM 39:17

*— Hail Mary —*

And Jesus said: Father, forgive them, for they
know not what they do. /
But they, dividing his garments, cast lots.
                                         LUKE 23:34

*— Hail Mary —*

For the word of the Lord is right, and all his
works are *done* with faithfulness. /
the earth is full of the mercy of the Lord.
PSALM 32:4, 5B

— *Hail Mary* —


And they put over his head his cause written: /
THIS IS JESUS THE KING OF THE JEWS.
MATTHEW 27:37

— *Hail Mary* —


That in the name of Jesus every knee should
bow, of those that are in heaven, on earth,
and under the earth: /
And that every tongue should confess that the
Lord Jesus Christ is in the glory of God the
Father.          PHILIPPIANS 2:10-11

— *Hail Mary* —


And the people stood beholding, and the rulers
with them derided him, saying: /
He saved others; let him save himself, if he be
Christ, the elect of God.      LUKE 23:35

— *Hail Mary* —

---

Let the heavens rejoice, and the earth be glad: /
and let them say among the nations:
   The Lord . . . reigned.
                         1 PARALIPOMENON 16:31

— *Hail Mary* —


. . . Jesus therefore had seen his mother and
   the disciple standing whom he loved, /
And from that hour, the disciple took her
   to his own.               JOHN 19:26A, 27B

— *Hail Mary* —


. . . Save us, O God our saviour: and gather us
   together, and deliver us from the nations, /
that we may give glory to thy holy name, and
   may rejoice in singing thy praises.
                         1 PARALIPOMENON 16:35

— *Hail Mary* —


— *Glory Be* —

# Wednesday's Glorious Mysteries

# *Wednesday's First Glorious Mystery*
## THE RESURRECTION

— *Our Father* —

And behold there was a great earthquake. For an
   angel of the Lord descended from heaven, /
and coming, rolled back the stone, and sat
   upon it.                          MATTHEW 28:2

— *Hail Mary* —


Thine, O Lord, is magnificence, and power,
   and glory, /
and victory: and to thee is praise:
                          1 PARALIPOMENON 29:11A

— *Hail Mary* —


And the angel answering, said to the women:
   Fear not you; for I know that you seek Jesus
   who was crucified. /

---

He is not here, for he is risen, as he said. Come, and see the place where the Lord was laid.

MATTHEW 28:5-6

*— Hail Mary —*


for all that is in heaven, and in earth, is thine: /
thine is the kingdom, O Lord, and thou art above all princes.

1 PARALIPOMENON 29:11B

*— Hail Mary —*


And they went out quickly from the sepulchre with fear and great joy, /
running to tell his disciples.

MATTHEW 28:8

*— Hail Mary —*


Thine are riches, and thine is glory, in thy hand is power and might: /
in thy hand greatness, and the empire of all things.

1 PARALIPOMENON 29:12A, C

*— Hail Mary —*

And behold Jesus met them, saying: All hail. /
But they came up and took hold of his feet,
   and adored him.         MATTHEW 28:9

*— Hail Mary —*


Now therefore our God we give thanks to thee, /
  and we praise thy glorious name.

1 PARALIPOMENON 29:13

*— Hail Mary —*


Then Jesus said to them: Fear not.
   Go, tell my brethren /
that they go into Galilee, there they shall
   see me.        MATTHEW 28:10

*— Hail Mary —*


O Lord God of Abraham, and of Isaac, and
   of Israel our fathers, keep for ever this will
   of their heart, /
and let this mind remain always for the
   worship of thee.    1 PARALIPOMENON 29:18

*— Hail Mary —*


*— Glory Be —*

# *Wednesday's Second Glorious Mystery*
## THE ASCENSION

— *Our Father* —

And the eleven disciples went into Galilee, /
  unto the mountain where Jesus had appointed
  them.                                 MATTHEW 28:16

— *Hail Mary* —

The Lord God is my strength: and he will make
  my feet like the feet of harts: /
and he the conqueror will lead me upon my
  high places singing psalms.

HABACUC 3:19

— *Hail Mary* —

And he said to them: These are the words which
  I spoke to you, while I was yet with you, /

that all things must needs be fulfilled, which
   are written in the law of Moses, and in the
   prophets, and in the psalms, concerning me.

LUKE 24:44

*— Hail Mary —*

Come ye to him and be enlightened: /
   and your faces shall not be confounded.

PSALM 33:6

*— Hail Mary —*

And he led them out as far as Bethania: /
   and lifting up his hands, he blessed them.

LUKE 24:50

*— Hail Mary —*

Let all thy works, O Lord, praise thee: /
   and let thy saints bless thee.

PSALM 144:10

*— Hail Mary —*

And Jesus coming, spoke to them, saying: /
All power is given to me in heaven and in
    earth.                 MATTHEW 28:18

*— Hail Mary —*


O magnify the Lord with me; /
and let us extol his name together.

                          PSALM 33:4

*— Hail Mary —*


And he said to them: Go ye into the whole
    world, /
and preach the gospel to every creature.

                        MARK 16:15

*— Hail Mary —*


O taste, and see that the Lord is sweet: /
for there is no want to them that fear him.

              PSALM 33:9A,10B

*— Hail Mary —*

*— Glory Be —*

# *Wednesday's Third Glorious Mystery*
## THE DESCENT OF THE HOLY SPIRIT

*— Our Father —*

And when the days of the Pentecost were
  accomplished, /
  they were all together in one place:

ACTS 2:1

*— Hail Mary —*

adore ye the Lord in his holy court. /
  Let all the earth be moved at his presence.

PSALM 95:9

*— Hail Mary —*

And suddenly there came a sound from heaven,
  as of a mighty wind coming, /
  and it filled the whole house where they were
  sitting.

ACTS 2:2

*— Hail Mary —*

O hear my prayer: all flesh shall come to thee. /
We shall be filled with the good things of thy
    house; holy is thy temple,

PSALM 64:3, 5B

— *Hail Mary* —


And there appeared to them parted tongues as it
    were of fire, /
and it sat upon every one of them:     ACTS 2:3

— *Hail Mary* —


God is in the midst thereof, it shall not be
    moved: /
Come and behold ye the works of the Lord:

PSALM 45:6A, 9A

— *Hail Mary* —


And they were all filled with the Holy [Spirit]*,
    and they began to speak with [diverse]**
    tongues, /
according as the Holy [Spirit]* gave them to
    speak.     ACTS 2:4

— *Hail Mary* —

---

* "Ghost" in the original translation     * * "divers" in the original translation

I cried to him with my mouth: /
and I extolled him with my tongue.

PSALM 65:17

*— Hail Mary —*


Now there were dwelling at Jerusalem, Jews,
 devout men, out of every nation under
 heaven. /
And they were all amazed, and wondered,
 saying: Behold, are not all these, that speak,
 Galileans?                                    ACTS 2:5, 7

*— Hail Mary —*


Give glory to the Lord, ye children of Israel, /
and praise him in the sight of the Gentiles:

TOBIAS 13:3

*— Hail Mary —*

*— Glory Be —*

# Wednesday's Fourth Glorious Mystery

## The Assumption

— *Our Father* —

*Behold my servant whom I have chosen, /*
*my beloved...*         Matthew 12:18a

— *Hail Mary* —

Thou art great, O Lord, for ever, /
and thy kingdom is unto all ages:

          Tobias 13:1b

— *Hail Mary* —

The fig tree ... put forth her green figs: the
vines in flower yield their sweet smell. /
Arise, my love, my beautiful one, and come:

         Canticle of Canticles 2:13

— *Hail Mary* —

And I and my soul will rejoice in him. /
  Bless ye the Lord, all his elect, keep days of joy,
    and give glory to him.          TOBIAS 13:9-10
              — *Hail Mary* —


Thou art all fair, O my love, /
  and there is not a spot in thee.
                    CANTICLE OF CANTICLES 4:7
              — *Hail Mary* —


Nations from afar shall come to thee: /
  For they shall call upon the great name in thee.
                          TOBIAS 13:14A, 15
              — *Hail Mary* —


What manner of one is thy beloved of the
    beloved, /
  O thou most beautiful among women?
                    CANTICLE OF CANTICLES 5:9A
              — *Hail Mary* —

Give glory to the Lord for thy good things, and
bless the God eternal, that he may rebuild his
tabernacle in thee, /
and may call back all the captives to thee, and
thou . . . rejoice for ever and ever.

TOBIAS 13:12

*— Hail Mary —*


Arise, be enlightened, O Jerusalem: for thy light
is come, /
and the glory of the Lord is risen upon thee.

ISAIAS 60:1

*— Hail Mary —*


Blessed are all they that love thee, /
and that rejoice in thy peace.

TOBIAS 13:18

*— Hail Mary —*

*— Glory Be —*

# Wednesday's Fifth Glorious Mystery
## THE CORONATION

*— Our Father —*

And a great sign appeared in heaven: A woman
  clothed with the sun, /
and the moon under her feet, and on her head
  a crown of twelve stars:    APOCALYPSE 12:1
*— Hail Mary —*


Begin ye to the Lord with timbrels, sing ye to
  the Lord with cymbals, /
tune unto him a new psalm, extol and call
  upon his name.          JUDITH 16:2
*— Hail Mary —*


She will render him good, and not evil, /
all the days of her life.      PROVERBS 31:12
*— Hail Mary —*

Let all thy creatures serve thee: /
and there is no one that can resist thy voice.

JUDITH 16:17A, C

*— Hail Mary —*


She . . . opened her hand to the needy, /
and stretched out her hands to the poor.

PROVERBS 31:20

*— Hail Mary —*


O hear my prayer: /
all flesh shall come to thee.          PSALM 64:3

*— Hail Mary —*


Strength and beauty are her clothing, /
and she shall laugh in the latter day.

PROVERBS 31:25

*— Hail Mary —*


But they that fear thee, /
shall be great with thee in all things.

JUDITH 16:19

*— Hail Mary —*

---

Many daughters have gathered together riches: /
thou . . . surpassed them all.

PROVERBS 31:29

*— Hail Mary —*

O magnify the Lord with me; /
and let us extol his name together.

PSALM 33:4

*— Hail Mary —*

*— Glory Be —*

# Thursday's Luminous Mysteries

# *Thursday's First Luminous Mystery*
## THE LORD'S BAPTISM IN THE JORDAN

— *Our Father* —

John was in the desert baptizing, /
  and preaching the baptism of penance, unto
    remission of sins.                    MARK 1:4

— *Hail Mary* —

We will praise thee, O God: we will praise, /
  and we will call upon thy name. We will relate
    thy wondrous works:              PSALM 74:2

— *Hail Mary* —

And it came to pass, in those days, Jesus came
    from Nazareth of Galilee, /
  and was baptized by John in the Jordan.
                                    MARK 1:9

— *Hail Mary* —

The mountains shall be moved from the
   foundations with the waters: /
the rocks shall melt as wax before thy face.

JUDITH 16:18

— *Hail Mary* —

And forthwith coming up out of the water, he
   saw the heavens opened, /
and the Spirit as a dove descending, and
   remaining on him.          MARK 1:10

— *Hail Mary* —

And the spirit of the Lord shall rest upon him:
   the spirit of wisdom, and of understanding, /
the spirit of counsel, and of fortitude, the spirit
   of knowledge, and of godliness.

ISAIAS 11:2

— *Hail Mary* —

And there came a voice from heaven: /
Thou art my beloved Son; in thee I am well
   pleased.          MARK 1:11

— *Hail Mary* —

---

Let mount Sion rejoice, and the daughters of
   Juda be glad; /
because of thy judgments, O Lord.

PSALM 47:12

*— Hail Mary —*

And immediately the Spirit /
   drove him out into the desert.

MARK 1:12

*— Hail Mary —*

For this is God, our God unto eternity,
   and for ever and ever: /
he shall rule us for evermore.

PSALM 47:15

*— Hail Mary —*

*— Glory Be —*

### *Thursday's Second Luminous Mystery*

## The Lord's Self-Manifestation at the Wedding of Cana

— *Our Father* —

And the third day, there was a marriage in
  Cana of Galilee: and the mother of Jesus was
  there. /
And Jesus also was invited, and his disciples, to
  the marriage.                          JOHN 2:1-2

— *Hail Mary* —


Send forth flowers, as the lily, and yield a smell,
  and bring forth leaves in grace, /
and praise with canticles, and bless the Lord in
  his works.                    ECCLESIASTICUS 39:19

— *Hail Mary* —

And the wine failing, the mother of Jesus saith
to him: They have no wine. /
And Jesus . . . to her: Woman, what is that to
me and to thee? my hour is not yet come.
JOHN 2:3-4

*— Hail Mary —*

Magnify his name, and give glory to him with
the voice of your lips, /
and with the canticles of your mouths.
ECCLESIASTICUS 39:20A

*— Hail Mary —*

Now there were set there six waterpots of stone,
according to the manner of the purifying of
the Jews, containing two or three measures
apiece. /
Jesus saith to them: Fill the waterpots with
water. And they filled them up to the brim.
JOHN 2:6-7

*— Hail Mary —*

The memory of him shall not depart away, /

and his name shall be in request from
   generation to generation.
                          ECCLESIASTICUS 39:13

   *— Hail Mary —*


And when the chief steward had tasted the
   water made wine, and knew not whence it
   was, And saith to him: /
Every man at first setteth forth good wine, and
   when men have well drunk, then that which
   is worse. But thou . . . kept the good wine
   until now.                    JOHN 2:9A, 10

   *— Hail Mary —*


At his word the waters stood as a heap: /
   and at the words of his mouth the receptacles
   of waters:               ECCLESIASTICUS 39:22

   *— Hail Mary —*


This beginning of miracles did Jesus in Cana of
   Galilee; /
and manifested his glory, and his disciples
   believed in him.               JOHN 2:11

   *— Hail Mary —*

---

All the works of the Lord are good, /
 and he will furnish every work in due time.

ECCLESIASTICUS 39:39

*— Hail Mary —*

*— Glory Be —*

# *Thursday's Third Luminous Mystery*

## THE LORD PROCLAIMS THE KINGDOM OF GOD AND CALLS US TO CONVERSION

*— Our Father —*

And after that John was delivered up, Jesus came into Galilee, preaching the gospel of the kingdom of God, /
And saying: The time is accomplished, and the kingdom of God is at hand: repent, and believe the gospel.        MARK 1:14-15

*— Hail Mary —*

For I am not ashamed of the gospel. /
For it is the power of God unto salvation . . .
                                                ROMANS 1:16

*— Hail Mary —*

Jesus answered: Amen, amen I say to thee,
   unless a man be born again /
of water and the Holy [Spirit]*, he cannot enter
   into the kingdom of God.          JOHN 3:5
          — *Hail Mary* —


For you are all the children of God /
  by faith, in Christ Jesus.

                              GALATIANS 3:26

          — *Hail Mary* —


That which is born of the flesh, is flesh; /
  and that which is born of the Spirit, is spirit.

                              JOHN 3:6

          — *Hail Mary* —


For as many of you as have been baptized in
   Christ, /
have put on Christ.          GALATIANS 3:27

          — *Hail Mary* —


For God sent not his Son into the world, to
   judge the world, /

                    * "Ghost" in the original translation

---

but that the world may be saved by him.

JOHN 3:17

*— Hail Mary —*

For by grace you are saved through faith, and
that not of yourselves, /
for it is the gift of God;                    EPHESIANS 2:8

*— Hail Mary —*

After these things Jesus and his disciples came
into the land of Judea: /
and there he abode with them, and baptized.

JOHN 3:22

*— Hail Mary —*

Now to him who is able to do all things more
abundantly than we desire or understand, /
To him be glory in the church, and in Christ
Jesus unto all generations, world without
end. Amen.                    EPHESIANS 3:20A, 21

*— Hail Mary —*

*— Glory Be —*

---

# *Thursday's Fourth Luminous Mystery*
## THE LORD'S TRANSFIGURATION

— *Our Father* —

he took Peter, and James, and John, and went
up into a mountain to pray. /
and his raiment became white and glittering.

LUKE 9:28B, 29B

— *Hail Mary* —

*Thy throne, O God, is for ever and ever: /
a sceptre of justice is the sceptre of thy kingdom.*

HEBREWS 1:8B-C

— *Hail Mary* —

And behold two men were talking with him.
And they were Moses and Elias, /

Appearing in majesty. And they spoke of his decease that he should accomplish in Jerusalem.                LUKE 9:30-31

*— Hail Mary —*

I will give praise to thee, O Lord, among the people: /
I will sing a psalm to thee among the nations.
PSALM 56:10

*— Hail Mary —*

But Peter and they that were with him were heavy with sleep. /
And waking, they saw his glory, and the two men that stood with him.        LUKE 9:32

*— Hail Mary —*

Be thou exalted, O God, above the heavens: /
and thy glory above all the earth.
PSALM 56:12

*— Hail Mary —*

Master, it is good for us to be here; and let us make three tabernacles, /

one for thee, and one for Moses, and one for
  Elias; not knowing what he said.

LUKE 9:33B

— *Hail Mary* —

Every valley shall be exalted, and every
  mountain and hill shall be made low. . . /
And the glory of the Lord shall be revealed.

ISAIAS 40:4A, 5A

— *Hail Mary* —

And as he spoke these things, there came a
  cloud, and overshadowed them; /
And a voice came out of the cloud, saying:
  This is my beloved Son; hear him.

LUKE 9:34A, 35

— *Hail Mary* —

Behold the Lord God shall come with strength,
  and his arm shall rule: /
Behold his reward is with him and his work is
  before him.

ISAIAS 40:10

— *Hail Mary* —

— *Glory Be* —

---

# *Thursday's Fifth Luminous Mystery*

## THE LORD'S INSTITUTION OF THE EUCHARIST AS THE SACRAMENTAL EXPRESSION OF THE PASCHAL MYSTERY

— *Our Father* —

And when the hour was come, he sat down, and
the twelve apostles with him. /
And he said to them: With desire I have desired
to eat this pasch with you, before I suffer.
LUKE 22:14-15

— *Hail Mary* —

He shall feed his flock like a shepherd: /
he shall gather together the lambs with his arm,
ISAIAS 40:11A

— *Hail Mary* —

And having taken the chalice, he gave thanks,
   and said: Take, and divide *it* among you: /
For I say to you, that I will not drink of the
   fruit of the vine, till the kingdom of God
   come.                               LUKE 22:17-18

— *Hail Mary* —


For thee my soul . . . thirsted; for thee my
   flesh, /
O how many ways!                       PSALM 62:2B

— *Hail Mary* —


And taking bread, he gave thanks . . . and gave
   to them, saying: /
This is my body, which is given for you. Do
   this for a commemoration of me.
                                       LUKE 22:19

— *Hail Mary* —


so in the sanctuary have I come before thee, /
to see thy power and thy glory.
                                       PSALM 62:3B

— *Hail Mary* —

---

In like manner the chalice also, after he had
supped, saying: /
This is the chalice, the new testament in my
blood, which shall be shed for you.

LUKE 22:20

*— Hail Mary —*


Let my soul be filled as with marrow and
fatness: /
and my mouth shall praise thee with
joyful lips.                                       PSALM 62:6

*— Hail Mary —*


For from the rising of the sun even to the going
down, my name is great among the Gentiles,
and in every place there is sacrifice, /
and there is offered to my name a clean
oblation: for my name is great among the
Gentiles. . .                              MALACHIAS 1:11

*— Hail Mary —*

Be still and see that I am God; I will be exalted
among the nations, /
and I will be exalted in the earth.

PSALM 45:11

*— Hail Mary —*

*— Glory Be —*

# Friday's
## Sorrowful Mysteries

# *Friday's First Sorrowful Mystery*
## THE AGONY IN THE GARDEN

*— Our Father —*

And his sweat became as drops of blood, /
  trickling down upon the ground.

LUKE 22:44

*— Hail Mary —*

Hear, O God, my supplication: be attentive to
  my prayer. /
So will I sing a psalm to thy name for ever and
  ever:

PSALM 60:2, 9A

*— Hail Mary —*

And when he rose up from prayer, and was
  come to his disciples, /
he found them sleeping for sorrow.

LUKE 22:45

*— Hail Mary —*

---

My heart is ready, O God, my heart is ready: /
Arise, O my glory, arise psaltery and harp:
   I will arise early.          PSALM 56:8A, 9
       *— Hail Mary —*


Watch ye, and pray that you enter not into
   temptation. /
The spirit indeed is willing, but the flesh is
   weak.                MARK 14:38
       *— Hail Mary —*


he shall not faint, nor labour, /
   neither is there any searching out of his
   wisdom.            ISAIAS 40:28B
       *— Hail Mary —*


As he was yet speaking, behold a multitude; and
   he that was called Judas, one of the twelve, /
went before them, and drew near to Jesus, for
   to kiss him.           LUKE 22:47
       *— Hail Mary —*

I will give praise to thee, O Lord, among the
    people: /
I will sing a psalm to thee among the nations.

PSALM 56:10

*— Hail Mary —*

Rise up, let us go. /
Behold, he that will betray me is at hand.

MARK 14:42

*— Hail Mary —*

But they that hope in the Lord shall renew their
    strength, they shall take wings as eagles, /
they shall run and not be weary, they shall walk
    and not faint.

ISAIAS 40:31

*— Hail Mary —*

*— Glory Be —*

---

# Friday's Second Sorrowful Mystery
## THE SCOURGING AT THE PILLAR

— *Our Father* —

Then therefore, Pilate took Jesus, /
and scourged him.     JOHN 19:1

— *Hail Mary* —

For I reckon that the sufferings of this time are
not worthy to be compared /
with the glory to come, that shall be revealed
in us.     ROMANS 8:18

— *Hail Mary* —

As many have been astonished at thee, so shall
his visage be inglorious among men, /
and his form among the sons of men.
    ISAIAS 52:14

— *Hail Mary* —

O the depth of the riches of the wisdom and of
the knowledge of God! /
How incomprehensible are his judgments, and
how unsearchable his ways!

ROMANS 11:33

*— Hail Mary —*


Surely he hath borne our infirmities and carried
our sorrows: /
and we have thought him as it were a leper, and
as one struck by God and afflicted.

ISAIAS 53:4

*— Hail Mary —*


What shall we then say to these things? /
If God be for us, who is against us?

ROMANS 8:31

*— Hail Mary —*


But he was wounded for our iniquities, he was
bruised for our sins: /
the chastisement of our peace was upon him,
and by his bruises we are healed.

ISAIAS 53:5

*— Hail Mary —*

I beseech you therefore, brethren, by the mercy
   of God, /
that you present your bodies a living sacrifice,
   holy, pleasing unto God, your reasonable
   service.                                ROMANS 12:1

   *— Hail Mary —*


by his knowledge shall this my just servant
   justify many, /
and he shall bear their iniquities.
                                        ISAIAS 53:11B

   *— Hail Mary —*


For it is written: *As I live . . . every knee shall bow
   to me, /
and every tongue shall confess to God.*
                                        ROMANS 14:11

   *— Hail Mary —*


   *— Glory Be —*

# *Friday's Third Sorrowful Mystery*
## THE CROWNING WITH THORNS

— *Our Father* —

And they blindfolded him, and smote his face.
  And they asked him, saying: /
Prophesy, who is it that struck thee?

LUKE 22:64

— *Hail Mary* —

For as the heavens are exalted above the earth,
  so are my ways exalted above your ways, /
and my thoughts above your thoughts.

ISAIAS 55:9

— *Hail Mary* —

And blaspheming, /
  many other things they said against him.

LUKE 22:65

— *Hail Mary* —

. . . Keep ye judgment, and do justice: /
for my salvation is near to come, and my
    justice to be revealed.          ISAIAS 56:1

— *Hail Mary* —


And as soon as it was day, the ancients of the
    people, and the chief priests and scribes,
    came together; /
and they brought him into their council, saying
    If thou be the Christ, tell us.

                                    LUKE 22:66

— *Hail Mary* —


The heavens declared his justice: /
and all people saw his glory.      PSALM 96:6

— *Hail Mary* —


And if I shall also ask you, you will not answer
    me, nor let me go. /
But hereafter the Son of man shall be sitting on
    the right hand of the power of God.

                                 LUKE 22:68-69

— *Hail Mary* —

For thou art the most high Lord over all the
   earth: /
thou art exalted exceedingly above all gods.

PSALM 96:9

*— Hail Mary —*

Then said they all: Art thou then the Son of
   God? /
Who said: You say that I am.

LUKE 22:70

*— Hail Mary —*

The stone which the builders rejected; the same
   is become the head of the corner. /
This is the Lord's doing: and it is wonderful in
   our eyes.

PSALM 117:22-23

*— Hail Mary —*

*— Glory Be —*

# *Friday's Fourth Sorrowful Mystery*
## THE CARRYING OF THE CROSS

*— Our Father —*

He was offered because it was his own will, and
he opened not his mouth: he shall be led as a
sheep to the slaughter, /
and shall be dumb as a lamb before his shearer,
and he shall not open his mouth.
ISAIAS 53:7

*— Hail Mary —*

All the ends of the earth shall remember, and
shall be converted to the Lord: /
And all the kindreds of the Gentiles shall adore
in his sight. PSALM 21:28

*— Hail Mary —*

He was taken away from distress, and from
judgment: who shall declare his generation? /

because he is cut off out of the land of the
living: for the wickedness of my people have
I struck him.                              ISAIAS 53:8
— *Hail Mary* —


For the word of the cross, to them indeed that
perish, is foolishness; /
but to them that are saved, that is, to us, it is
the power of God.          1 CORINTHIANS 1:18
— *Hail Mary* —


And the Lord was pleased to bruise him in
infirmity: if he shall lay down his life for
sin, /
he shall see a long-lived seed, and the will of
the Lord shall be prosperous in his hand.
                                           ISAIAS 53:10
— *Hail Mary* —


His seed shall be mighty upon earth: /
the generation of the righteous shall be blessed.
                                           PSALM 111:2
— *Hail Mary* —

And he said to all: If any man will come after me, /
let him deny himself, and take up his cross
   daily, and follow me.                    LUKE 9:23
         *— Hail Mary —*


For you are bought with a great price. /
   Glorify and bear God in your body.
                              1 CORINTHIANS 6:20

         *— Hail Mary —*


And bearing his own cross, he went forth to
   that place which is called Calvary, /
but in Hebrew Golgotha.                    JOHN 19:17
         *— Hail Mary —*


Yet to us there is but one God, the Father, of
   whom are all things, and we unto him; /
and one Lord Jesus Christ, by whom are all
   things, and we by him.
                              1 CORINTHIANS 8:6

         *— Hail Mary —*


         *— Glory Be —*

# *Friday's Fifth Sorrowful Mystery*
## THE CRUCIFIXION

*— Our Father —*

Now from the sixth hour there was darkness
over the whole earth, /
until the ninth hour.     MATTHEW 27:45

*— Hail Mary —*

Clouds and darkness *are* round about him: /
justice and judgment *are* the establishment of
his throne.     PSALM 96:2

*— Hail Mary —*

And about the ninth hour Jesus cried with a
loud voice, saying: Eli, Eli, lamma
sabacthani? /
that is, My God, my God, why hast thou
forsaken me?     MATTHEW 27:46

*— Hail Mary —*

---

But the Lord is the true God: he is the living
  God, and the everlasting king: /
at his wrath the earth shall tremble, and the
  nations shall not be able to abide his
  threatening.                          JEREMIAS 10:10

— *Hail Mary* —


And Jesus crying with a loud voice, said: Father,
  into thy hands I commend my spirit. /
And saying this, he gave up the ghost.
                                        LUKE 23:46

— *Hail Mary* —


When my soul was in distress within me, I
  remembered the Lord: /
that my prayer may come to thee, unto thy
  holy temple.
                                        JONAS 2:8

— *Hail Mary* —

And the centurion who stood over against him,
    seeing that crying out in this manner he had
    given up the ghost, said: /
Indeed this man was the son of God.

MARK 15:39

*— Hail Mary —*


Give ye glory to the Lord your God, before it be
    dark, and before your feet stumble upon the
    dark mountains: /
  you shall look for light, and he will turn it into
    the shadow of death, and into darkness.

JEREMIAS 13:16

*— Hail Mary —*


And Joseph taking the body, wrapped it up in a
    clean linen cloth. And laid it in his own new
    monument, /
  which he had hewed out in a rock. And he
    rolled a great stone to the door of the
    monument, and went his way.

MATTHEW 27:59-60

*— Hail Mary —*

---

I went down to the lowest parts of the
   mountains: the bars of the earth have shut
   me up for ever: /
and thou wilt bring up my life from
   corruption, O Lord my God.       JONAS 2:7

   — *Hail Mary* —

   — *Glory Be* —

# Saturday's Joyful Mysteries

# *Saturday's First Joyful Mystery*
## THE ANNUNCIATION

*— Our Father —*

Therefore the Lord himself shall give you a sign.
Behold a virgin shall conceive, /
and bear a son, and his name shall be called
Emmanuel.                                    ISAIAS 7:14

*— Hail Mary —*

Bring ye to the Lord, O ye kindreds of the
Gentiles, bring ye to the Lord glory and
honour: /
bring to the Lord glory unto his name.
                                              PSALM 95:7-8A

*— Hail Mary —*

And Mary said to the angel: How shall this
be done, /
because I know not man?              LUKE 1:34

*— Hail Mary —*

---

Know ye that the Lord he is God: /
he made us, and not we ourselves.

PSALM 99:3A

*— Hail Mary —*

And the angel answering, said to her: The Holy
  [Spirit]* shall come upon thee, and the power
  of the most High shall overshadow thee. /
And therefore also the Holy which shall be
  born of thee shall be called the Son of God.

LUKE 1:35

*— Hail Mary —*

Who shall declare the powers of the Lord? /
who shall set forth all his praises?

PSALM 105:2

*— Hail Mary —*

And behold thy cousin Elizabeth, she also . . .
  conceived a son in her old age; /
and this is the sixth month with her that is
  called barren:

LUKE 1:36-37

*— Hail Mary —*

---

* "Ghost" in the original translation

Praise the Lord, ye children: praise ye the name
    of the Lord. /
Blessed be the name of the Lord, from
    henceforth now and for ever.

PSALM 112:1-2

*— Hail Mary —*

And Mary said: Behold the handmaid of the
    Lord; /
be it done to me according to thy word.
    And the angel departed from her.

LUKE 1:38

*— Hail Mary —*

My heart is ready, O God, my heart is ready: /
I will sing, and will give praise, with my glory.

PSALM 107:2

*— Hail Mary —*

*— Glory Be —*

---

# Saturday's Second Joyful Mystery
## THE VISITATION

*— Our Father —*

And Mary said: /
My soul doth magnify the Lord.

LUKE 1:46

*— Hail Mary —*

And my spirit . . . rejoiced /
in God my Saviour.          LUKE 1:47

*— Hail Mary —*

Because he . . . regarded the humility of his
    handmaid; /
for behold . . . all generations shall call me
    blessed.          LUKE 1:48

*— Hail Mary —*

Because he that is mighty, hath done great
   things to me; /
and holy is his name.      LUKE 1:49
   *— Hail Mary —*


And his mercy is from generation unto
   generations, /
to them that fear him.      LUKE 1:50
   *— Hail Mary —*


he . . . scattered the proud /
in the conceit of their heart.      LUKE 1:51B
   *— Hail Mary —*


He . . . put down the mighty from their seat, /
and . . . exalted the humble.      LUKE 1:52
   *— Hail Mary —*


He . . . filled the hungry with good things; /
and the rich he . . . sent empty away.
     LUKE 1:53
   *— Hail Mary —*

---

He . . . received Israel his servant, being mindful
of his mercy: /
As he spoke to our fathers, to Abraham and to
his seed for ever.                     LUKE 1:54-55

— *Hail Mary* —


And Mary abode with her about three
months; /
and she returned to her own house.
                                       LUKE 1:56

— *Hail Mary* —

— *Glory Be* —

# *Saturday's Third Joyful Mystery*
## THE NATIVITY

*— Our Father —*

*Behold a virgin shall be with child, and bring
  forth a son, /
and they shall call his name Emmanuel,* which
  being interpreted is, *God with us.*

MATTHEW 1:23

*— Hail Mary —*

The Lord is the keeper of little ones: /
I was humbled, and he delivered me.

PSALM 114:6

*— Hail Mary —*

And there were in the same country shepherds
  watching, and keeping the night watches
  over their flock. /

---

And behold an angel of the Lord stood by
  them, and the brightness of God shone
  round about them; and they feared with a
  great fear.                    LUKE 2:8-9
— *Hail Mary* —

To the righteous a light is risen up in darkness: /
*he is* merciful, and compassionate and just.
                               PSALM 111:4
— *Hail Mary* —

And the angel said to them: Fear not; for,
  behold, I bring you good tidings of great joy,
  that shall be to all the people: /
For, this day, is born to you a Saviour, who is
  Christ the Lord, in the city of David.
                               LUKE 2:10-11
— *Hail Mary* —

Thy name, O Lord, is for ever: /
  thy memorial, O Lord, unto all generations.
                               PSALM 134:13
— *Hail Mary* —

---

And this shall be a sign unto you. /
You shall find the infant wrapped in swaddling
   clothes, and laid in a manger.       LUKE 2:12
       *— Hail Mary —*


O Lord, my might, and my strength, /
 and my refuge in the day of tribulation:
                              JEREMIAS 16:19A
       *— Hail Mary —*


And suddenly there was with the angel a
   multitude of the heavenly army, praising
   God, and saying: /
Glory to God in the highest; and on earth peace
   to men of good will.       LUKE 2:13-14
       *— Hail Mary —*


And now they that are redeemed by the Lord,
   shall return, and shall come into Sion singing
   praises, /

and joy everlasting *shall be* upon their heads,
they shall obtain joy and gladness, sorrow
and mourning shall flee away.     ISAIAS 51:11

— *Hail Mary* —

— *Glory Be* —

# Saturday's Fourth Joyful Mystery
## THE PRESENTATION

— *Our Father* —

And his father and mother were wondering at
those things /
which were spoken concerning him.

LUKE 2:33

— *Hail Mary* —

Give praise, O daughter of Sion: shout,
O Israel: /
the king of Israel the Lord *is* in the midst of
thee . . .

SOPHONIAS 3:14A, 15B

— *Hail Mary* —

And Simeon blessed them, and said to Mary his
mother: Behold this *child* is set for the fall, /

and for the resurrection of many in Israel, and
for a sign which shall be contradicted;
LUKE 2:34

*— Hail Mary —*

The Lord thy God in the midst of thee *is*
mighty, he will save: he will rejoice over thee
with gladness, /
he will be silent in his love, he will be joyful
over thee in praise.    SOPHONIAS 3:17

*— Hail Mary —*

And thy own soul a sword shall pierce, /
that, out of many hearts, thoughts may be
revealed.    LUKE 2:35

*— Hail Mary —*

And who shall know thy thought, except thou
give wisdom, /
and send thy Holy Spirit from above:
WISDOM 9:17

*— Hail Mary —*

And there was one Anna, a prophetess . . . /
who departed not from the temple, by fastings
and prayers serving night and day.

LUKE 2:36A, 37B

— *Hail Mary* —

I cried to him with my mouth: /
and I extolled him with my tongue.

PSALM 65:17

— *Hail Mary* —

Now she, at the same hour, coming in,
confessed to the Lord; /
and spoke of him to all that looked for the
redemption of Israel.               LUKE 2:38

— *Hail Mary* —

But I will rejoice in the Lord: /
and I will joy in God my Jesus.

HABACUC 3:18

— *Hail Mary* —

— *Glory Be* —

# *Saturday's Fifth Joyful Mystery*

## THE FINDING OF JESUS IN THE TEMPLE

*— Our Father —*

And seeing *him,* they wondered. And his
    mother said to him: /
behold thy father and I have sought thee
    sorrowing.             LUKE 2:48A, C

*— Hail Mary —*

For a thousand years in thy sight *are* as
    yesterday, which is past. /
And as a watch in the night,     PSALM 89:4

*— Hail Mary —*

And he said to them: How is it that you sought
    me? /
did you not know, that I must be about my
    father's business?         LUKE 2:49

*— Hail Mary —*

And let the brightness of the Lord our God be
    upon us: /
and direct thou the works of our hands over us;
                                    PSALM 89:17A-B

— *Hail Mary* —


And they understood not the word /
    that he spoke unto them.          LUKE 2:50
                — *Hail Mary* —


O Lord, how great are thy works! /
    thy thoughts are exceeding deep.

                                        PSALM 91:6

                — *Hail Mary* —


And he went down with them, and came to
    Nazareth, and was subject to them. /
And his mother kept all these words in her
    heart.                          LUKE 2:51
                — *Hail Mary* —

---

All ye works of the Lord, bless the Lord: /
praise and exalt him above all for ever.

DANIEL 3:57

*— Hail Mary —*

And Jesus advanced in wisdom, /
and age, and grace with God and men.

LUKE 2:52

*— Hail Mary —*

They that are planted in the house of the Lord /
shall flourish in the courts of the house of our
God.

PSALM 91:14

*— Hail Mary —*

*— Glory Be —*

# Sunday's Glorious Mysteries

# *Sunday's First Glorious Mystery*
## THE RESURRECTION

*— Our Father —*

Now when it was late that same day, the first of
the week, and the doors were shut, where the
disciples were gathered together, for fear of
the Jews, /
Jesus came and stood in the midst, and said to
them: Peace be to you. JOHN 20:19

*— Hail Mary —*

O how good and sweet is thy spirit, /
O Lord, in all things! WISDOM 12:1

*— Hail Mary —*

And seeing him they adored: /
but some doubted. MATTHEW 28:17

*— Hail Mary —*

---

*but thou art the selfsame, /*
*and thy years shall not fail.*

HEBREWS 1:12B

*— Hail Mary —*


He said therefore to them again: Peace be to
  you. /
As the Father . . . sent me, I also send you.

JOHN 20:21

*— Hail Mary —*


That he might make known unto us the
  mystery of his will, /
to re-establish all things in Christ, that are in
  heaven and on earth, in him.

EPHESIANS 1:9A, 10B

*— Hail Mary —*


When he had said this, he breathed on them; /
and he said to them: Receive ye the
  Holy [Spirit]*.

JOHN 20:22

*— Hail Mary —*

---

* "Ghost" in the original translation

In whom you also, after you had heard the word
of truth . . . you were signed with the holy
Spirit of promise, /
Who is the pledge of our inheritance, unto the
praise of his glory.
EPHESIANS 1:13A, C; 14A, C

*— Hail Mary —*


Whose sins you shall forgive, they are forgiven
them; /
and whose *sins* you shall retain, they are
retained. JOHN 20:23

*— Hail Mary —*


Now to him who is able to do all things more
abundantly than we desire or understand . . . /
To him be glory in the church, and in Christ
Jesus unto all generations, world without
end. Amen. EPHESIANS 3:20A, 21

*— Hail Mary —*


*— Glory Be —*

# Sunday's Second Glorious Mystery
## THE ASCENSION

*— Our Father —*

And Jesus coming, spoke to them, saying: All
power is given to me in heaven and in
earth. /

Going therefore, teach ye all nations; baptizing
them in the name of the Father, and of the
Son, and of the Holy [Spirit]*.

MATTHEW 28:18-19

*— Hail Mary —*

And he is the head of the body, the church, who
is the beginning, /

the firstborn from the dead; that in all things
he may hold the primacy:

COLOSSIANS 1:18

*— Hail Mary —*

---

* "Ghost" in the original translation

And he said to them: These are the words which
    I spoke to you, while I was yet with you, that
    all things must needs be fulfilled, /
which are written in the law of Moses, and
    in the prophets, and in the psalms,
    concerning me.                              LUKE 24:44

— *Hail Mary* —


For in him were all things created in heaven and
    on earth, visible and invisible, /
whether thrones, or dominations, or
    principalities, or powers: all things were
    created by him and in him.
                                        COLOSSIANS 1:16

— *Hail Mary* —


But you shall receive the power of the Holy
    [Spirit]* coming upon you, and you shall be
    witnesses unto me in Jerusalem, /
and in all Judea, and Samaria, and even to the
    uttermost part of the earth.          ACTS 1:8

— *Hail Mary* —


* "Ghost" in the original translation

And you are filled in him, /
who is the head of all principality and power:

COLOSSIANS 2:10

*— Hail Mary —*

And when he had said these things, while they
looked on, /
he was raised up: and a cloud received him out
of their sight.

ACTS 1:9

*— Hail Mary —*

Therefore, if you be risen with Christ, seek the
things that are above; /
where Christ is sitting at the right hand of
God:

COLOSSIANS 3:1

*— Hail Mary —*

And while they were beholding him going up to
heaven, behold two men stood by them in
white garments. /
Who also said . . . This Jesus who is taken up
from you into heaven, shall so come, as you
have seen him going into heaven.

ACTS 1:10-11

*— Hail Mary —*

When Christ shall appear, who is your life, /
then you also shall appear with him in glory.
COLOSSIANS 3:4

*— Hail Mary —*

*— Glory Be —*

# Sunday's Third Glorious Mystery
## THE DESCENT OF THE HOLY SPIRIT

*— Our Father —*

But Peter standing up with the eleven, lifted up
his voice, and spoke to them: /
But this is that which was spoken of by the
prophet Joel:               ACTS 2:14A, 16
*— Hail Mary —*


Generation and generation shall praise thy
works: /
and they shall declare thy power.    PSALM 144:4
*— Hail Mary —*


*And it shall come to pass, in the last days . . . I
will pour out of my Spirit upon all flesh: /
and your sons and your daughters shall prophesy,
and your young men shall see visions, and your
old men shall dream dreams.*        ACTS 2:17
*— Hail Mary —*

They shall speak of the magnificence of the
  glory of thy holiness: /
and shall tell thy wondrous works.

PSALM 144:5

*— Hail Mary —*

Being exalted therefore by the right hand of
  God, and having received of the Father the
  promise of the Holy [Spirit]*, /
he ... poured forth this which you see and
  hear.

ACTS 2:33

*— Hail Mary —*

They shall speak of the glory of thy kingdom: /
and shall tell of thy power:   PSALM 144:11

*— Hail Mary —*

But Peter *said* to them: Do penance, and be
  baptized every one of you in the name of
  Jesus Christ, /
for the remission of your sins: and you shall
  receive the gift of the Holy [Spirit].

ACTS 2:38

*— Hail Mary —*

* "Ghost" in the original translation

---

To make thy might known to the sons of men: /
and the glory of the magnificence of thy
    kingdom.                     PSALM 144:12

*— Hail Mary —*


For the promise is to you, and to your children,
    and to all that are far off, /
whomsoever the Lord our God shall call.
                              ACTS 2:39

*— Hail Mary —*


Thy kingdom is a kingdom of all ages: /
to all that call upon him in truth.
                 PSALM 144:13A, 18B

*— Hail Mary —*


*— Glory Be —*

# *Sunday's Fourth Glorious Mystery*
## THE ASSUMPTION

— *Our Father* —

For I know that my Redeemer liveth, /
and in the last day I shall rise out of the earth.

JOB 19:25

— *Hail Mary* —

Great is our Lord, and great is his power: /
and of his wisdom there is no number.

PSALM 146:5

— *Hail Mary* —

And I shall be clothed again with my skin, /
and in my flesh I shall see my God.

JOB 19:26

— *Hail Mary* —

My mouth shall speak the praise of the Lord: /
and let all flesh bless his holy name for ever;
   yea, for ever and ever.          PSALM 144:21

   — *Hail Mary* —


And the temple of God was opened in heaven:
   and the ark of his testament was seen in his
   temple, /
and there were lightnings, and voices, and an
   earthquake, and great hail.
                              APOCALYPSE 11:19

   — *Hail Mary* —


And every creature, which is in heaven, and on
   the earth, and under the earth, and such as
   are in the sea, and all that are in them: I
   heard all saying: /
To him . . . on the throne, and to the Lamb,
   benediction, and honour, and glory, and
   power, for ever and ever.
                              APOCALYPSE 5:13

   — *Hail Mary* —

For the Lord himself shall come down from
heaven with commandment, and with the
voice of an archangel, /
and with the trumpet of God: and the dead
who are in Christ, shall rise first.

1 Thessalonians 4:15

— *Hail Mary* —

Let all flesh be silent at the presence of the
Lord: /
for he is risen up out of his holy habitation.

Zacharias 2:13

— *Hail Mary* —

Then we who are alive, who are left, shall be
taken up together with them in the clouds to
meet Christ, into the air, /
and so shall we be always with the Lord.
Wherefore, comfort ye one another with
these words.

1 Thessalonians 4:16-17

— *Hail Mary* —

... Benediction, and glory, and wisdom, and
    thanksgiving, honour, /
and power, and strength to our God for ever
    and ever. Amen.

APOCALYPSE 7:12

*— Hail Mary —*

*— Glory Be —*

# *Sunday's Fifth Glorious Mystery*
## THE CORONATION

*— Our Father —*

Favour is deceitful, and beauty is vain: /
the woman that feareth the Lord, she shall be
praised. PROVERBS 31:30

*— Hail Mary —*

Great and wonderful are thy works, O Lord
God Almighty; /
just and true are thy ways, O King of ages.
APOCALYPSE 15:3B

*— Hail Mary —*

Give her of the fruit of her hands: /
and let her works praise her in the gates.
PROVERBS 31:31

*— Hail Mary —*

Who shall not fear thee, /
O Lord, and magnify thy name?

APOCALYPSE 15:4A

*— Hail Mary —*

To him that shall overcome, I will give to sit
with me in my throne: /
as I also have overcome, and am set down with
my Father in his throne.

APOCALYPSE 3:21

*— Hail Mary —*

After these things I heard as it were the voice of
much people in heaven, saying: /
Alleluia. Salvation, and glory, and power is to
our God.

APOCALYPSE 19:1

*— Hail Mary —*

And whosoever shall exalt himself shall be
humbled: /
and he that shall humble himself shall be
exalted.

MATTHEW 23:12

*— Hail Mary —*

And a voice came out from the throne, saying:
    Give praise to our God, /
all ye his servants; and you that fear him, little
    and great. APOCALYPSE 19:5

— *Hail Mary* —


Be thou faithful until death: /
    and I will give thee the crown of life.
        APOCALYPSE 2:10C

— *Hail Mary* —


And he said to me: Write: Blessed are they /
    that are called to the marriage supper of the
        Lamb. APOCALYPSE 19:9A

— *Hail Mary* —


— *Glory Be* —

# *Appendix A:*

## PRAYERS OF THE ROSARY

**APOSTLES' CREED**
I believe in God, the Father almighty, creator of heaven and earth; and in Jesus Christ, his only Son, our Lord; who was conceived by the Holy Spirit, born of the Virgin Mary; suffered under Pontius Pilate, was crucified, died, and was buried. He descended into hell; the third day he arose again from the dead. He ascended into heaven, and is seated at the right hand of God the Father almighty; from thence he shall come to judge the living and the dead. I believe in the Holy Spirit, the holy catholic Church, the communion of saints, the forgiveness of sins, the resurrection of the body, and life everlasting. Amen.

**OUR FATHER**
Our Father, who art in heaven, hallowed be thy name. Thy kingdom come. Thy will be done, on earth as it is in heaven. Give us this day our daily

bread; and forgive us our trespasses as we forgive those who trespass against us; and lead us not into temptation, but deliver us from evil. Amen.

## HAIL MARY
Hail Mary, full of grace, the Lord is with thee; blessed art thou among women, and blessed is the fruit of thy womb, Jesus. Holy Mary, Mother of God, pray for us sinners, now and at the hour of our death. Amen.

## GLORY BE
Glory be to the Father, and to the Son, and to the Holy Spirit; as it was in the beginning, is now, and ever shall be, world without end. Amen.

## FATIMA PRAYER
O my Jesus, forgive us our sins, save us from the fires of hell, and lead all souls to heaven, especially those most in need of thy mercy.

(Note: Commonly prayed after each Glory Be.)

## HAIL HOLY QUEEN
Hail, Holy Queen, Mother of mercy! Hail, our life, our sweetness, and our hope! To thee do we

---

cry, poor banished children of Eve; to thee do we send up our sighs, mourning and weeping in this valley of tears! Turn then, most gracious advocate, thine eyes of mercy toward us; and after this, our exile, show unto us the blessed fruit of thy womb, Jesus. O clement, O loving, O sweet Virgin Mary!

Pray for us, O Holy Mother of God.
That we may be made worthy of the promises of Christ.

(Note: It is very fitting to say the Hail Holy Queen at the end of the Rosary.)

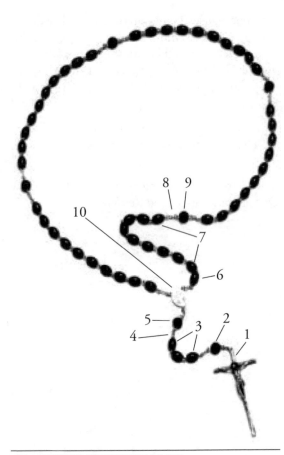

# *Appendix B:*

## HOW TO PRAY THE ROSARY

1. After making the Sign of the Cross, say the Apostles' Creed.
2. Say the Our Father.
3. Say three Hail Marys.
4. Say the Glory Be.
5. Announce the first mystery, then say the Our Father.
6. Read the first Scripture excerpt, then say the first Hail Mary while meditating on the mystery.
7. Repeat Step 6 for the nine remaining Hail Marys in the decade.
8. Say the Glory Be.
9. Announce the second mystery, then say the Our Father. Repeat Steps 6, 7, and 8 and continue with the third, fourth, and fifth mysteries in the same manner.
10. While not essential, it is very fitting to say the Hail Holy Queen at the end of the Rosary, then kiss the cross and make the Sign of the Cross.

# The Salvation Novena
## An Advent Scriptural Rosary

### The Salvation Novena
By Larry London
0-87973-**917**-7, paper, 136 pp.

Larry London helps us prepare for the Lord's Second Coming by combining the serenity of the Rosary with meditations on the mysteries of salvation and the Incarnation to create a new novena.

*Available at bookstores. Credit card customers can order direct from* **Our Sunday Visitor** *by calling* **1-800-348-2440, ext. 3**. *Order online at www.osv.com.*

## Our Sunday Visitor

200 Noll Plaza • Huntington, IN 46750

A39BBABP

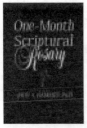

## Our Sunday Visitor ...
### *Your Source for Discovering the Riches of the Catholic Faith*

Our Sunday Visitor has an extensive line of materials for young children, teens, and adults. Our books, Bibles, booklets, CD-ROMs, audios, and videos are available in bookstores worldwide.

To receive a FREE full-line catalog or for more information, call **Our Sunday Visitor** at **1-800-348-2440, ext. 3**. Or write, **Our Sunday Visitor** / 200 Noll Plaza / Huntington, IN 46750.

------------------------------------------------------------

Please send me ___ A catalog
Please send me materials on:
___ Apologetics and catechetics
___ Prayer books
___ The family
___ Reference works
___ Heritage and the saints
___ The parish
Name _____
Address _____ Apt. _____
City _____ State _____ Zip _____
Telephone ( ) _____

A39BBABP

------------------------------------------------------------

Please send a friend ___ A catalog
Please send me materials on:
___ Apologetics and catechetics
___ Prayer books
___ The family
___ Reference works
___ Heritage and the saints
___ The parish
Name _____
Address _____ Apt. _____
City _____ State _____ Zip _____
Telephone ( ) _____

A39BBABP

**OurSundayVisitor**

200 Noll Plaza, Huntington, IN 46750
Toll free: **1-800-348-2440**
Website: www.osv.com